CW01271221

WHAT CAN WE DO?

INEQUALITY

KATIE DICKER

W
FRANKLIN WATTS
LONDON • SYDNEY

First published in Great Britain in 2023 by Hodder & Stoughton
Copyright © Hodder & Stoughton, 2023

Produced for Franklin Watts by
White-Thomson Publishing Ltd
www.wtpub.co.uk

All rights reserved.

Editor: Katie Dicker
Series Designer: Dan Prescott

HB ISBN: 978 1 4451 8795 2
PB ISBN: 978 1 4451 8796 9
Ebook ISBN: 978 1 4451 8797 6

Franklin Watts
An imprint of
Hachette Children's Group
Part of Hodder & Stoughton
Carmelite House
50 Victoria Embankment
London EC4Y 0DZ

An Hachette UK Company
www.hachette.co.uk
www.hachettechildrens.co.uk

MIX
Paper from responsible sources
FSC® C104740

Printed in Dubai

Picture acknowledgements:
Shutterstock: Daniel Samray *cover t*, Andrei Armiagov *cover b*, Irina Boldina 4, Kordin Viacheslav 5, humphery 6, arindambanerjee 8, Jenson 9, Monkey Business Images 10 and 13, panoglobe 11, Michal Urbanek 12, timsimages.uk 14, De Visu 16, Fabio Michele Capelli 17t, Finn stock 17b, Quality Stock Arts 20, Miaron Billy 21, Holli 23, Parinya.Maneenate 24, VisualArtStudio 25, maroke 26, hrui 28, ChaitanyaChadha 29; Getty: Jeff Vinnick / Stringer 7, Kate Green / Stringer 15t, Ed Giles / Stringer 15b; Alamy: Olivier Asselin 18, Abaca Press 19, REUTERS 22, Hemis 27.

All design elements from Shutterstock.

Every effort has been made to clear copyright. Should there be any inadvertent omission, please apply to the publisher for rectification.

The website addresses (URLs) included in this book were valid at the time of going to press. However, it is possible that contents or addresses may have changed since the publication of this book. No responsibility for any such changes can be accepted by either the author or the publisher.

All facts and statistics were correct at the time of press.

CONTENTS

What is inequality?	4
Inequality of opportunity	6
Inequality between countries	8
Inequality within countries	10
The racial gap	12
The gender gap	14
The generation gap	16
The health gap	18
The tech gap	20
The super-rich	22
The effects of inequality	24
Global action	26
Even the odds	28
Glossary	30
Further information	31
Index	32

WHAT IS INEQUALITY?

We are all unique human beings, with different talents and skills. As we go through life, our experiences shape who we are. But sometimes the different paths we take are caused by inequality – not being treated fairly. And this may affect how healthy, wealthy or educated we become.

Stereotypes

We can make assumptions about the people we meet, and this can cause us to treat them differently. In the workplace, for example, men may be given more responsibilities than women, an older employee may be overlooked for training, while a younger person may be given simpler tasks. Someone who can't speak the same language may be excluded from a social gathering if people assume they won't enjoy the conversation. It's important to challenge our assumptions.

There are over 200 different nationalities in the world and over 7,000 different languages. But we're all human beings, with a great deal in common.

Inequality of outcome

About 200 years ago, there was less inequality in the world – life was short wherever you lived and most people lived in poverty. But as countries began to develop, inequality grew between nations. And within those nations, different cultures, policies and laws meant that some groups of people were left behind. When people are richer or poorer than one another, or have different opportunities available to them, we call it 'inequality of outcome'. In this book we will look at different types of inequality and what we can do to make things fairer.

IT'S A FACT

In 2015, the United Nations (UN) set a series of 'sustainable development goals' to reach by 2030, with a central promise to 'leave no one behind'. Goal 10 was to reduce inequality within and among countries.

Inequality can cause people to have a very different standard of living, wherever they live in the world.

INEQUALITY OF OPPORTUNITY

In a fair world, people would be given the same life chances. We call this 'equality of opportunity'. Natural differences may then evolve because people have unique talents, or perhaps they work very hard for their achievements. But sometimes a different outcome is caused by an unfair advantage.

An electronics factory in China – now the second-largest economy in the world. China's success is partly due to the hard work of its citizens, with many goods now sold internationally.

Life incentives

'Equality of opportunity' is sometimes called a 'level playing field' (see page 7). It's a fair system where everyone is given the same chances but the 'best' people are still allowed to get ahead. When the system is fair, inequality of outcome can be a force for good, giving people a reason to work hard for a better life. If people earn more money, it also makes a country wealthier, which benefits everyone.

EQUALITY IN SPORT

Equality of opportunity can be seen in team sports where you change ends at half time in case the pitch is sloped or the Sun is dazzling, giving the same advantages and disadvantages to both teams. In some sports, a 'handicap' gives players of different abilities an equal chance of winning – better golfers need fewer shots on the course, for example, and successful horses carry more weight in horse racing. In the real world, taxation and other measures try to 'level the playing field' in society, trade and business, but it's not always easy.

Unfair advantage

It's difficult to give everyone a fair chance when people are born into different circumstances that affect their career opportunities and life choices. Perhaps someone is wealthier because they're more talented or they've worked harder. But they may have had a better education, more support from their family, more connections to ask for help or more money to pay for it. Talent alone doesn't explain why the world's richest one per cent of people own nearly half of the world's wealth.

The US has the most billionaires, including Microsoft-founder Bill Gates (left) and Amazon-founder Jeff Bezos (right). In recent years, the largest fortunes have been made in the tech industry.

INEQUALITY BETWEEN COUNTRIES

The simple fact of where you're born can affect your life chances. Countries use their populations and their natural resources to develop, but some regions are better-placed than others. Although global inequality has started to fall since the 1990s, the average income in the US is 16 times higher than in sub-Saharan Africa, where over 40 per cent of people live in extreme poverty.

Better chances

Some countries have more natural resources, more fertile land and a good climate for farming. It's easier to get ahead when you have the resources you need to pay for development and easy to fall behind if you're prone to natural disasters. Parts of Africa and Asia have rapidly growing populations, without the money or infrastructure needed to support them. Other countries are dealing with conflict or corrupt governments, stalling their chances of progress.

Earthquake damage in Haiti. Once a wealthy colony, political instability and natural disasters have seen a reverse in Haiti's fortunes and severely impacted its development.

Making money

To develop, countries need to export (sell abroad) more goods or services and reduce any debts. But it can be difficult to compete with large companies, or regions like Europe, the US and China, which account for nearly half of world trade. Many low-income nations are also paying interest on loans from other nations or private lenders. Recent economic growth in Asia has helped to lessen the gap between countries, but climate change is bringing new challenges. Tropical regions have many low-income countries dependent on the weather and farming for their livelihoods.

What Can I Do?

When you shop, look for fairtrade products that guarantee a price for farmers and support development in their region, and use customer feedback forms in stores to demand change. You could also raise funds for an international development charity by taking part in a sponsorship challenge.

High-income countries tend to produce high-value goods, such as cars, which bring a stable income. Low-income countries usually produce low-value primary products, such as food, which can fluctuate in price.

INEQUALITY WITHIN COUNTRIES

While the inequality gap between countries is starting to narrow, inequality within countries is on the rise. We see this type of inequality in run-down cities and deprived rural areas. Today, over 70 per cent of the world's population lives in countries where inequality has grown, particularly since the challenges of the Covid-19 pandemic.

Hospitality and retail businesses were badly affected by the Covid-19 pandemic. Governments tried to redress this with financial support for the worst off.

Changing fortunes

After the Second World War (1939–1945), inequality fell within high-income countries. This was because the richest people paid more taxes to help with war debts, more jobs became available and the creation of welfare states gave support to the most vulnerable. But in recent years, post-war funding has ceased, economic growth has slowed, and some jobs have been lost to technology or moved to the international market. The average income gap between the top 10 per cent and the bottom 50 per cent of people within countries has almost doubled in 20 years.

The rural-urban divide

Within nations, rural regions tend to have a lower income and less access to healthcare, education and employment. But cities have areas of deprivation, too. Governments in high-income nations are more able to invest in deprived areas, offering grants to support small businesses, improving infrastructure, and making housing more affordable. Equality of opportunity can also be affected by differences such as gender, age, ethnicity and religion. Governments try to address these issues, too, by funding community-based projects and supporting the needs of disadvantaged groups.

What Can I Do?

There are lots of things you can do to help reduce inequality in your local area:

- Encourage your family and friends to support new and local businesses.
- Donate unwanted goods to charity.
- Donate long-life produce to food banks that offer support to those in need.
- With the help of a parent or carer, get involved in some community fundraising and encourage friends to join in, too.

A high-voltage power line being constructed in a rural region in India. Access to electricity, sanitation and transport links is crucial for a region's development.

THE RACIAL GAP

For centuries, people have been treated differently because of the colour of their skin, their country of origin or their religion, and minorities have often been persecuted in favour of the majority. But as the world becomes more connected and people move to other regions to work or study, racial inequality has become more apparent.

Black Lives Matter

In the last decade, an international human rights movement called 'Black Lives Matter' (BLM) has highlighted the racism, discrimination and inequality experienced by black people in their daily lives. Initially formed in response to violent assaults at the hands of US police, the movement has also drawn attention to harassment, fewer educational and job opportunities, lower pay, less access to healthcare and unfair treatment before the law.

A Black Lives Matter rally in Vancouver, Canada. Since it was founded in 2013, the BLM movement has seen protests and demonstrations in many cities of the world.

Entrenched beliefs

Racial inequality is deeply rooted in the past. In the 17th and 18th centuries, for example, European colonies in the Americas enslaved African people and this led to the white culture being seen as normal or 'better'. Some people consider others to be 'outsiders' and oppose immigration because they think migrants take their jobs or use government funds, but immigration can bring skills and fill gaps in the workforce. Today, name-blind job applications can prevent an unconscious bias and positive action can give opportunities to applicants from disadvantaged groups.

What Can I Do?

Be open-minded, kind and respectful to the people you meet:

- Learn about other cultures and ways of life.
- Get involved in community groups such as sports clubs and music groups to meet different types of people.
- If you've experienced racism or observed it happening, always tell an adult you trust.

CHANGING TIMES

In South Africa, the legacy of slavery lived on in a form of segregation called 'apartheid' in which black and white people lived very separate lives. The minority white population were given a higher status in politics, in housing and the workplace. Apartheid was abolished in 1991 and South Africa had its first Black president, Nelson Mandela, in 1994. Although it takes time for attitudes to change, government policies such as BEE (Black Economic Empowerment) provide opportunities for black communities to grow and excel, to help redress the balance.

Initiatives like this community workshop now give opportunities for all races in South Africa to grow and develop their skills.

THE GENDER GAP

Throughout history, men and women have been treated differently and women have had to fight for equality – from property and voting rights to equality in the workplace and before the law. Although opportunities for women have increased dramatically in many parts of the world, there's still a lot of work to be done.

Family divide

Historically, girls were often educated to be wives and mothers, rather than to follow a career. Today, girls have more opportunities, but in some countries, girls still can't attend school because they need to work or care for family members. In the workplace, too, women often have low-skilled jobs with low wages, or jobs that are easy to fit around childcare or other unpaid caring responsibilities. Globally, women on average earn 16 per cent less than men, although in many places this figure is much higher. Afghanistan currently has the greatest gender pay gap.

Under Taliban rule, girls in Afghanistan can't go to secondary school and women have restricted working opportunities. Women have to wear a face covering in public and can't travel long distances alone.

MALALA YOUSAFZAI

When Malala Yousafzai was 11 years old, she wrote a blog about her life in Swat, Pakistan, under the Taliban regime, helping to raise awareness that girls like her were forbidden to go to school. Malala continued to fight for her right to an education and three years later, she was shot by Taliban soldiers who saw her as a threat to their regime. Malala's family moved to the UK where she recovered from her injuries and later launched a fund to help girls worldwide to receive an education.

In 2014, Malala Yousafzai became the youngest person to win the Nobel Peace Prize and she continues to campaign for women's education.

Voting rights

In the 20th century, women in many countries fought for the right to vote in elections to have a say in how their country was governed, and it wasn't until the late 1800s that many married women had the right to own or inherit property and to spend their earnings. Today, women have the right to vote in every region of the world, except Vatican City (where Catholic male cardinals elect the Pope). In practice, however, women's voting rights are often severely restricted.

In Egypt, you need an ID-card to vote at a polling station, but few women have one, and if they do, it's usually the property of their husband.

THE GENERATION GAP

The place of your birth can affect your life chances, but your opportunities can also depend on *when* you were born. Each generation has its own challenges to face – such as war, economic crises or climate change. Older and younger people can also be stereotyped in the media, and this can influence our views of people at different stages of life.

As technology moves on, some older people can feel excluded and left behind. We can all help by sharing our knowledge with older family members.

Old and young

Older people may be refused car insurance on the basis of age rather than risk, overlooked for training opportunities or made redundant from their jobs. People's perceptions of the elderly may cause them to be patronised or treated differently in public. On the other side, many young people earn less than their grandparents did at the same age. They may be unable to afford to buy a house or run a car and have less secure job opportunities. Inequality can exist within generations, too, with some people supported by their family's wealth.

Looking ahead

In 2015, Wales became the first country to include the protection of future generations in its laws. This inspired other nations to introduce long-term thinking in areas such as housing, taxation and employment. In 2019, New Zealand unveiled a Wellbeing Budget, to move the focus away from economic targets, towards tackling long-term challenges, such as child poverty and housing. Some nations are considering a universal grant to help young people to acquire new skills or to save for a house or a pension, and better funded technical education to support young people as career paths change.

Children in Italy join a Youth for Climate protest. This global initiative encourages young people to use their voice to call for more action on the climate crisis.

NEW BEGINNING

History has shown that it's possible for a country to reverse its fortunes. Finland, for example, used to be poor with a high mortality rate but today it's one of the healthiest and wealthiest countries in the world. Finland developed late, with rapid industrialisation after the Second World War (1939–1945). Examples like these are inspiring for low-income countries to see what can be achieved in a relatively short space of time.

Blue skies over Helsinki, the capital of Finland. Once an underdeveloped agricultural nation, Finland has become one of the world's economic leaders.

THE HEALTH GAP

Good health is something we take for granted, but access to healthcare is essential for a good quality of life. There are natural inequalities in health – women tend to live, on average, five years longer than men, for example, and our ethnicity can affect how susceptible we are to certain diseases. But health can also be affected by wealth and where we live.

Access to healthcare

Universal healthcare treats patients regardless of their income, but the wealthiest can still afford to live healthier lives. In low-income countries, 1 in 10 children are likely to die before the age of five, as opposed to 1 in 250 in high-income countries, while in São Paulo, Brazil, people in the richest areas can expect to live 14 years longer than those in the poorest parts. In high-income countries, there are more incidences of cancer linked to smoking and obesity in deprived areas. Cancer rates are lower in richer areas, and people tend to be diagnosed earlier, because they have more access to healthcare and are more likely to take up the offer of screening.

A woman waits with her baby at a health clinic in Sierra Leone. The country currently has one of the world's highest infant mortality rates.

Living with a disability

People with a disability often have poorer health outcomes and limited educational and employment opportunities. Where they can, governments offer benefits and financial support to help with additional costs. Increasingly, regulations try to make public spaces and services more accessible to all. This includes communication systems for sight-, hearing- or speech-impaired people. Technology can be a great help with this. Smartphone apps, for example, can work with braille displays or produce visual alerts and computer-generated speech.

THE VACCINE GAP

The Covid-19 pandemic deepened inequalities within and between nations, hitting the poorest hardest. Wealthier people were better equipped to deal with the challenges and high-income countries were more able to offer compensation and to quickly vaccinate their populations. In some countries, the poorest were nearly four times more likely to die from Covid-19 as the richest. In March 2020, the UN set up a Covid-19 Response and Recovery Fund to support low- and middle-income countries and the most vulnerable groups with the challenges ahead.

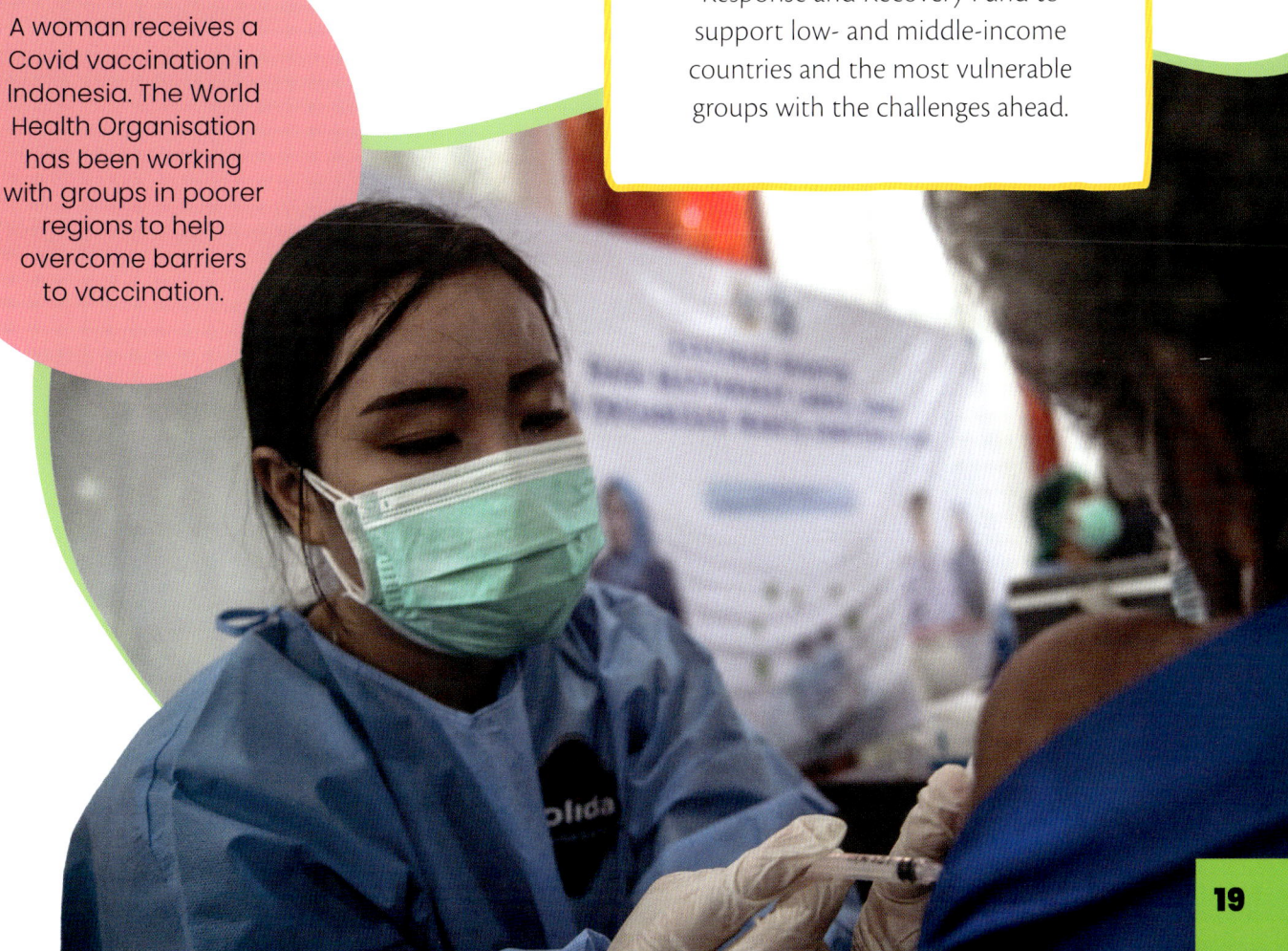

A woman receives a Covid vaccination in Indonesia. The World Health Organisation has been working with groups in poorer regions to help overcome barriers to vaccination.

THE TECH GAP

Technology can be a great leveller – it brings people together, makes the world feel like a smaller place and can provide near universal access to trade and services. During the Covid-19 pandemic, many businesses went online to survive. But in some parts of the world, mobile or Internet access is restricted, and some groups are being left behind.

E-commerce

When we buy or sell goods online, we call it e-commerce. This type of trade has helped businesses to grow and to keep costs down. Sellers can reach a wider audience and can reduce their costs of renting or repairing a store, and buyers can quickly and easily choose from a wide range of products. E-commerce is particularly beneficial to small businesses in remote regions. In a similar way, digital education has had far-reaching effects, changing many lives – providing you can get online.

We can learn so much online, from traditional studies to crafts, DIY tips and food recipes. But not everyone has access to the Internet.

Lack of access

In many parts of the world, people don't have a reliable or affordable Internet connection. Globally, around three billion people can't get online – mainly in rural, isolated communities in low-income countries. It can be difficult to get a business going when electricity supplies are limited, or postal services and road networks are unreliable. To help a country develop, governments try to invest in key areas, such as transport, energy, water and sanitation.

In Kenya, you can pay for goods and services, such as medicines from this pharmacy, through mobile money transfer.

MOBILE REVOLUTION

In Kenya in 2006, only 14 per cent of people had a bank account while more than 80 per cent of people had a mobile phone. 'Mobile money' was launched in 2007 so people could use their phones to buy products and services and to support their family and friends with cashflow. 'Mobile money' has improved the Kenyan economy and the efficiency of services. Kenya is now a world leader in the technology and is exporting the idea to other nations.

THE SUPER-RICH

Over the years, some families and individuals have become extremely wealthy. You may have heard of rich families such as the Waltons (Walmart) or the Mars family (Mars candy), or rich individuals like Elon Musk and Jeff Bezos. Extreme wealth can bring opportunities for all, but it can also have a damaging effect on our society.

Money talks

When someone becomes very wealthy it can have a 'trickle down' effect, perhaps because their business creates jobs, or they donate some of their wealth to charity. But extreme wealth can cause inequality to grow in unhealthy ways. Throughout history, the wealthiest people have often had the greatest power, being able to influence decisions. The rich may give donations to a political party, for example, to influence policies that are in their own interests – such as low taxation or lax business regulations, while bribery is an extreme example of wealthy people 'paying' for a favourable outcome.

In 2018, businessman Francisco Correa Sánchez was sentenced to 51 years in prison for bribing Spanish politicians to gain government contracts, in Spain's worst political corruption scandal.

Dangerous influence

It can be difficult for some groups to get their voices heard, while the super-rich can have a great influence. Many billionaires now own big media brands, including Elon Musk (Twitter), Jeff Bezos (*The Washington Post*) and Rupert Murdoch (multiple newspapers and news channels). Opponents say their wealth means they can extend their influence and support their own business interests. Misleading news stories or withheld information, for example, can influence the way people vote or think for themselves.

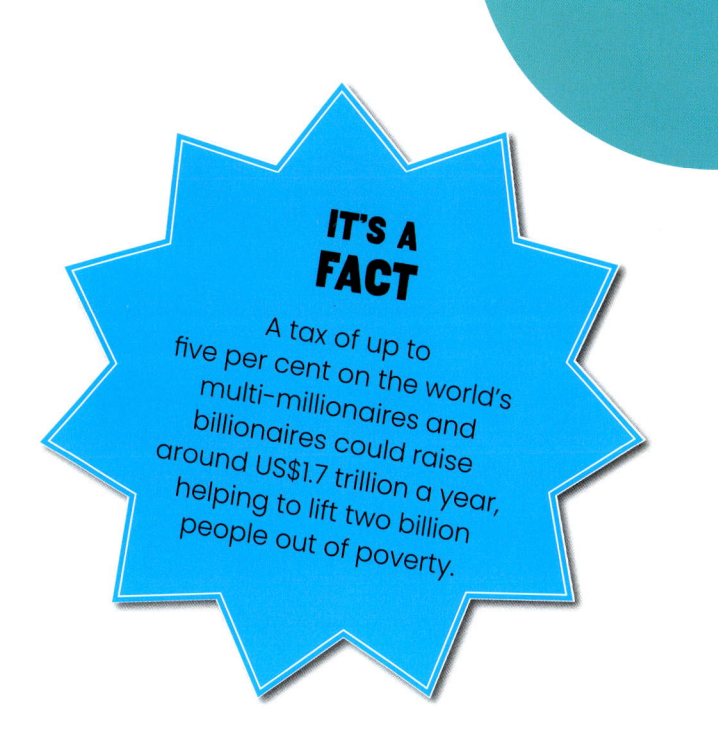

IT'S A FACT

A tax of up to five per cent on the world's multi-millionaires and billionaires could raise around US$1.7 trillion a year, helping to lift two billion people out of poverty.

In 2020, climate activists protested outside the News Corp Australia headquarters in Sydney against Rupert Murdoch's influence on media stories.

THE EFFECTS OF INEQUALITY

The inequalities we see around us have an impact on people's economic prospects and their general health and wellbeing. Inequality also has wider implications for countries, causing social unrest and economic decline. But it's possible to turn things around with government support, innovative thinking and collective action.

Personal impact

Inequality can affect people's happiness and sense of self-worth. Fewer educational and job opportunities can lead to less wealth, poorer health and a shorter lifespan. The effects are more acute in low-income countries, but the impact can be just as real in high-income countries, too. In these nations, only 75 per cent of children from the poorest families complete secondary education, compared to 90 per cent of children from the richest families. Governments try to invest in initiatives that make education more accessible for all.

Social inequality can affect your mental wellbeing if you feel you're less worthy than other people. Educational opportunities are a key area for gaining new skills and renewed confidence.

In Ontario, Canada, educational reforms have seen students performing well, whatever their socio-economic background or first language.

EDUCATION REVIVAL

In 2005, the province of Ontario, Canada, legally raised its school leaving age to 18 and introduced a range of incentives for students and teachers, such as a wider curriculum, innovative training and apprenticeship schemes. Nearly a third of school children in Canada come from migrant families, but a focus on equality helped to remove traditional barriers to their education. There has been a significant rise in attainment at all levels and Ontario's education system now ranks among the best in the world.

Wider impact

Inequality can also threaten long-term social and economic development. When people feel they've been treated unfairly they begin to lose trust in the government, and this can sometimes lead to crime and conflict. People may become more protective of their country and their jobs and resent the effects of globalisation, such as immigration. Political instability can also discourage foreign investment. Research has shown that less equal societies have less stable economies, which in turn can cause more inequality. It's in a government's interests to do all that it can to address this.

GLOBAL ACTION

In today's world, we're increasingly connected and global inequality affects us all. We need to take action to make the world a fairer place for everyone, but we also need to consider the unique circumstances of different countries and regions to get to the root causes of the problem.

Local support

Governments can use taxation to help redistribute wealth. A progressive tax system, for example, means the wealthiest individuals and companies pay the most, while windfall taxes can help to claw back extreme wealth that's been generated by unusual market conditions. Meanwhile, a publicly-funded benefits system can redistribute money to the most vulnerable. Norway, for example, has low levels of inequality, thanks to collective wage agreements and policies that support education and subsidise parenthood.

Governments can also sponsor job creation schemes and pass anti-discrimination laws. Actively seeking to bring diversity into political decisions can also help to redistribute influence and power.

Japan has low levels of inequality, due to high tax rates for the rich and for inheritance. In 2020, 'equal pay for equal work' regulations were introduced to protect part-time workers and to address gender inequality.

A helping hand

High-income countries can offer financial support to vulnerable nations. Global financial institutions such as the International Monetary Fund and the World Bank also offer development finance and assist countries in crisis. Trade rules and regulations can keep prices fair and trading agreements can bring more security to lower-income nations. As we move forward, we also need to give lower-income countries more say in global decision-making. At the UN Climate Change Conference in 2022, for example, nations from around the world agreed to a 'loss and damage' fund to help the vulnerable countries hardest hit by the effects of climate change.

What Can I Do?

Minorities can be under-represented or deliberately excluded from political decisions (if an address or ID-card is required to vote, for example). Signing a petition is one way you can show your support to under-represented groups. You can also write to your local representative to challenge decisions that worsen inequality, and demand changes that will improve it, such as equal pay, a fair living wage, windfall taxes on extreme wealth, anti-discrimination laws and foreign aid.

Sandbags help to prevent beach erosion in the Maldives, the majority of which lies less than a metre above rising sea levels. More sustainable solutions for low-lying regions include raising houses and creating artificial land.

EVEN THE ODDS

To give everyone a good chance in life, regardless of their circumstances, we need to find a balance between economic, social and environmental development, so that growth is sustainable and available to all. If we can all be more mindful of equality and inclusivity in our thoughts and actions, the world will be a fairer and happier place for everyone.

The root causes

To move forward, we need to identify who is being left behind and why, how to address the root causes of the problem, and how we can monitor and measure progress. We need to find a sustainable way to support our growing populations and to encourage equality of opportunity. Every person should have equal access to healthcare, education, employment, affordable housing and a stable income.

Governments need to adopt a forward-thinking approach to development, so their growth is sustainable and environmentally-sound for future generations.

Working together

We need to make extreme poverty a thing of the past. Low-income countries need opportunities to pay off their debts, or to cancel unmanageable payments, so they can develop and compete fairly on the world stage. Climate change has been exacerbated by the development of high-income nations and is now disproportionately affecting low-income countries. We need to do all we can to reduce our climate impact and to offer support. By funding development and economic growth, we can open up opportunities so that most people can benefit, rather than just a lucky few. Governments have the power to change laws, but change also begins in the community and we can all play our part.

This community kitchen in Gurugram, India, provides daily food for underprivileged people in the city, helping to improve their health and prospects.

UN DECLARATION OF HUMAN RIGHTS

In 1948, the UN adopted the Universal Declaration of Human Rights (UDHR) – 30 rights and freedoms that belong to us all and are protected by law – most notably that all humans are free and equal. On the tenth anniversary of the UDHR, Chair of the UN Human Rights Commission Eleanor Roosevelt spoke these words. Think about how they might be relevant to you and your community.

'Where, after all, do universal human rights begin? ... In the world of the individual person; the neighbourhood he lives in; the school or college he attends; the factory, farm, or office where he works. Such are the places where every man, woman, and child seeks equal justice, equal opportunity, equal dignity without discrimination.'

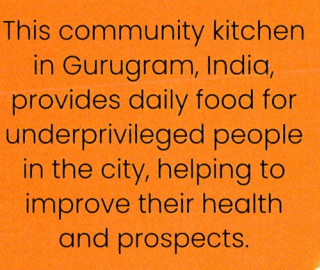

GLOSSARY

Americas The countries and territories of North America, Central America and South America.

bribery The offering or receiving of an item of value to influence the actions of an individual.

colony A country or region under the political control of another country and occupied by settlers from that country.

conflict A serious disagreement between nations or groups, such as fighting a war.

corrupt Acting dishonestly in return for money or personal gain.

Covid-19 pandemic An infectious disease that emerged in 2019 and spread around the world.

discrimination When someone is treated unfairly for being different, because of their race, age, gender or disability, for example.

economy The way a country or region spends and makes money.

ethnicity Belonging to a group that shares a common cultural background or descent.

exports Goods or services that a country sells to another country.

gender To be male, female or another identity.

globalisation The growing interdependence of countries, due to international trade, investment, technology and immigration.

immigration When people move to live permanently in another country.

infrastructure Transportation systems and communication networks, such as roads, railways, power supplies and Internet access.

International Monetary Fund An organisation that works to achieve sustainable growth and prosperity for its 190 member countries.

majority A large group of people that represent more than half of the total.

minority A small group of people that represent less than half of the total.

mortality A term used for the death rate.

positive action A policy in job applications that favours individuals belonging to disadvantaged groups, when they are of equal merit to other candidates.

sanitation Facilities that keep a place clean and free from infection, such as access to clean drinking water and sewage disposal.

sub-Saharan Africa An area of Africa that lies south of the Sahara Desert.

taxation Money that a government requires individuals to pay, depending on their income or wealth, to help fund its services.

United Nations An international organisation founded in 1945. Its 193 member states work together to maintain international peace, security and cooperation.

welfare state A system whereby a government protects the health and wellbeing of its citizens, especially the most vulnerable.

windfall tax A one-off tax on a company (or group of companies) who have made unusually high profits due to rare and unexpected market conditions.

World Bank An international organisation, with 189 member countries, that provides loans and grants to the governments of low- and middle-income nations to improve their economies.

FURTHER INFORMATION

Books

Stand Against: Prejudice by Izzi Howell, Franklin Watts, 2020

I'm a Global Citizen: We're All Equal by Georgia Amson-Bradshaw, Franklin Watts, 2020

17 Ways to Save the World by Louise Spilsbury, Franklin Watts, 2020

Websites

globalgoals.org/goals
Learn more about the UN's sustainable development goals.

worldslargestlesson.globalgoals.org
Fun activities and resources to help you make a difference.

dosomething.org/us/campaigns
Inspiring ideas to take action in your community.

INDEX

Afghanistan 14
Africa 8, 13, 18, 21
age 4, 11, 16–17
Asia 8, 9, 11, 19, 29
Australia 23

Bezos, Jeff 7, 22, 23
Black Lives Matter 12

Canada 12, 25
China 6, 9
climate change 9, 16, 17, 23, 27, 29
conflict 8, 16, 25
Correa Sánchez, Francisco 22
corruption 8, 22
Covid-19 pandemic 10, 19, 20

debts 9, 10, 29
development 5, 8, 9, 11, 17, 21, 25, 27, 28, 29
disability 19

education 4, 7, 11, 12, 14, 15, 17, 19, 20, 24, 25, 26, 28
Egypt 15
employment 4, 10, 11, 12, 13, 14, 16, 17, 19, 22, 24, 25, 26, 28, 29
equality of opportunity 6–7, 11, 28, 29
ethnicity 4, 11, 12–13, 18
Europe 9, 13, 17, 22, 26
exports 9, 21

fairtrade 9
farming 8, 9, 17, 29

Finland 17
food 9, 11, 20, 29

Gates, Bill 7
gender 4, 11, 14–15, 18, 26

Haiti 8
health 4, 11, 12, 17, 18–19, 24, 28, 29
healthcare 11, 12, 18, 19, 28
high-income countries 9, 10, 11, 18, 19, 24, 27, 29
housing 11, 13, 17, 28
human rights 12, 29

immigration 13, 25
income 8, 9, 10, 11, 12, 14, 16, 18, 27, 28
India 11, 29
inequality of opportunity 6–7
inequality of outcome 5, 6, 19
infrastructure 8, 11, 20, 21
International Monetary Fund 27

Japan 26

Kenya 21

language 4, 25
laws 5, 12, 14, 15, 17, 26, 27, 29
low-income countries 9, 17, 18, 19, 21, 24, 27, 29

middle-income countries 19, 27
minorities 12, 13, 27
Murdoch, Rupert 23
Musk, Elon 22, 23

natural disasters 8
New Zealand 17
Norway 26

population growth 8, 28
poverty 5, 8, 17, 19, 23, 29

race (see ethnicity)
religion 11, 12
rural 10, 11, 20, 21

Second World War 10, 17
social unrest 24, 25
South Africa 13
Spain 22
stereotypes 4, 16
sub-Saharan Africa 8

taxation 7, 10, 17, 22, 23, 26, 27
technology 7, 10, 16, 19, 20–21
trade 7, 9, 20, 27

United Nations 5, 19, 27, 29
United States 7, 8, 9
urban 10, 11

voting rights 14, 15, 27

Wales 17
wealth 4, 5, 6, 7, 8, 16, 17, 18, 19, 22–23, 24, 26, 27
welfare states 10, 19, 26
World Bank 27
World Health Organisation 19

Yousafzai, Malala 15

WHAT CAN WE DO?

TITLES IN THE SERIES

CLIMATE CHANGE
- What is climate change?
- Taking action
- Changing weather
- The Amazon Rainforest
- Melting ice
- Ocean impact
- Energy for buildings
- The food we eat
- The way we travel
- Shopping habits
- The power of tech
- Reduce, repair, reuse, recycle
- Speaking out

DISEASE
- What is disease?
- Communicable diseases
- Non-communicable diseases
- Cancer
- Cardiovascular diseases
- Chronic respiratory diseases
- Diabetes
- Viral diseases
- Bacterial diseases
- Parasitic diseases
- Vaccination
- Public health and sanitation
- The future of disease

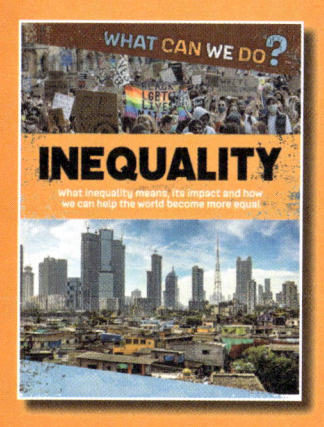

INEQUALITY
- What is inequality?
- Inequality of opportunity
- Inequality between countries
- Inequality within countries
- The racial gap
- The gender gap
- The generation gap
- The health gap
- The tech gap
- The super-rich
- The effects of inequality
- Global action
- Even the odds

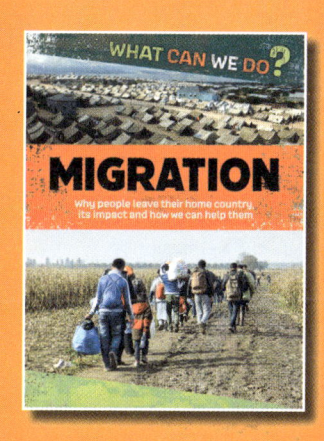

MIGRATION
- What is migration?
- Why do people migrate?
- Who are migrants and where do they go?
- Fleeing danger: refugees and IDPs
- How moving is good for migrants
- Difficulties for migrants
- How migration helps host countries
- Problems for host countries
- Helping their homelands
- Brain drain and dependence
- Building peace
- Climate change action
- The debate – freedom of movement

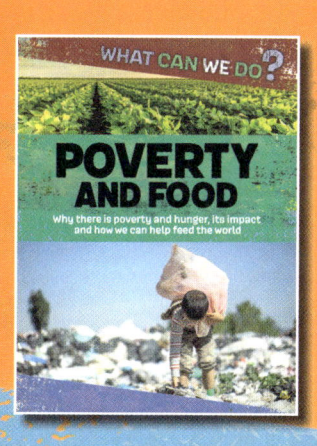

POVERTY AND FOOD
- What is poverty?
- What causes poverty?
- Rising prices
- What is food insecurity?
- Food supplies
- Tackling food waste
- Famine
- Regional variance
- The rural-urban divide
- Costs and consequences
- Caring for crops
- International cooperation
- A sustainable future

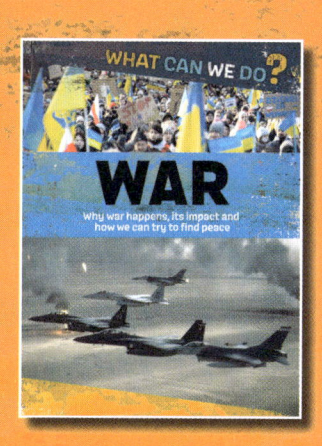

WAR
- What are war and conflict?
- How wars break out
- Fighting wars
- The impact on soldiers
- The impact on civilians
- Nuclear weapons
- The rules of war
- The United Nations
- Responses to war
- Safe zones
- Talking peace
- Rebuilding trust